Red Line 5

Vokabellernheft

Herausgeber: Dr. Frank Haß

Ernst Klett Verlag
Stuttgart • Leipzig

Liebe Schülerin, lieber Schüler,

mit diesem Vokabellernheft im praktischen Taschenformat kannst du überall deine Wörter lernen, wiederholen und nachschlagen.
In den Wortlisten kannst du Wörter und Wendungen, die dir schwierig vorkommen, mit Textmarker oder Bleistift markieren, um sie dann immer wieder durchzugehen.
Auch die vielen Übungen nach jeder Unit unterstützen dich bei der Wiederholung. So kannst du dich prima auf Vokabeltests vorbereiten.

In den Übungen, die mit diesem Zeichen ● gekennzeichnet sind, übst du die blau gedruckten Wörter.

Hinter jedem Wort ist die Lautschrift (z. B. [kəʊ'ɑːlə] für *Koala*) angegeben. Diese hilft dir, wenn du nicht weißt, wie du das Wort aussprechen sollst.
Hilfreiche Hinweise zum Umgang mit den Lautschriftzeichen findest du **in deinem Englischbuch** ab Seite 213 am unteren Rand aller *Dictionary*-Seiten.

Viel Erfolg beim Vokabellernen!

Zoom in

p. 8	**ladies and gentlemen** [ˌleɪdiz‿ən ˈdʒentlmən]	meine Damen und Herren

Unit 1 Exploring Australia

p. 10	to **explore** [ɪk'splɔ:]	erkunden; erforschen

Way in

p. 10	**Australian** [ɒs'treɪliən]	Australier; Australierin; australisch
	easy-going [ˌi:zi'gəʊɪŋ]	gelassen; locker
	continent ['kɒntɪnənt]	Kontinent; Erdteil
	Antarctica [æn'tɑ:ktɪkə]	Antarktis
	koala [kəʊ'ɑ:lə]	Koala
p. 11	to **emigrate** ['emɪgreɪt]	auswandern
	carpenter ['kɑ:pəntə]	Zimmermann; Zimmerin; Tischler; Tischlerin
	nurse [nɜ:s]	Krankenschwester; Krankenpfleger
	Aboriginal people [æbəˌrɪdʒnl 'pi:pl]	die Aborigines
	disease [dɪ'zi:z]	Krankheit; Infektionskrankheit
	to **struggle** ['strʌgl]	kämpfen; ringen; sich anstrengen; Mühe haben
	few [fju:]	wenige
	the outback [ði 'aʊtbæk]	Outback *(australisches Hinterland)*
	satellite dish ['sætlaɪt ˌdɪʃ]	Satellitenschüssel
	necessary ['nesəsri]	nötig; notwendig; erforderlich
	station ['steɪʃn]	Farm *(in Australien)*
	to **look forward to (+ -ing)** [ˌlʊk 'fɔ:wəd tə]	sich freuen auf
	boarding school ['bɔ:dɪŋ ˌsku:l]	Internat

Station 1

Respect

respectful [rɪ'spektfl]	respektvoll
ignorant ['ɪgnərnt]	ignorant; unwissend
to **ignore** [ɪg'nɔ:]	ignorieren; außer Acht lassen
respect [rɪ'spekt]	Respekt
politeness [pə'laɪtnəs]	Höflichkeit
rude [ru:d]	unhöflich; unverschämt
rudeness ['ru:dnəs]	Unhöflichkeit; Unverschämtheit
acceptable [ək'septəbl]	akzeptabel; annehmbar
tolerance ['tɒlrns]	Toleranz
acceptance [ək'septəns]	Akzeptanz; Zustimmung
tolerant ['tɒlrnt]	tolerant
ignorance ['ɪgnərns]	Ignoranz
disrespect [ˌdɪsrɪ'spekt]	Respektlosigkeit
disrespectful [ˌdɪsrɪ'spektfl]	respektlos

p. 12	**sacred** ['seɪkrɪd]	heilig
	view [vju:]	Aussicht; Sicht; Ausblick; Blick
	university [ˌju:nɪ'vɜ:səti]	Universität
	tour guide ['tʊə ˌgaɪd]	Reiseleiter; Reiseleiterin
	to **send in** [send‿'ɪn]	einschicken; einsenden
	application [ˌæplɪ'keɪʃn]	Bewerbung
	creature ['kri:tʃə]	Kreatur; Lebewesen; Geschöpf
	belief [bɪ'li:f]	Glaube; Überzeugung
	meaning ['mi:nɪŋ]	Bedeutung
	to **behave** [bɪ'heɪv]	sich benehmen; sich verhalten
	path [pɑ:θ]	Pfad; Weg

	desert ['dezət]	Wüste
	camel ['kæml]	Kamel
	behaviour [bɪ'heɪvjə]	Verhalten
p. 13	**closed** [kləʊzd]	geschlossen
	priest [pri:st]	Priester
	to **realise** ['rɪəlaɪz]	erkennen; realisieren
	to **take off** [ˌteɪk‿'ɒf]	abnehmen; ausziehen; herunternehmen
p. 14	to **look up** [ˌlʊk‿'ʌp]	nachschlagen; nachschauen
p. 15	**climb** [klaɪm]	Aufstieg
	seat [si:t]	Sitz; Sitzplatz

Station 2

Jobs

receptionist [rɪ'sepʃnɪst]	Empfangschef; Empfangschefin
electrician [ˌelɪk'trɪʃn]	Elektriker; Elektrikerin
travel agent ['trævl‿ˌeɪdʒnt]	Reisebürokaufmann; Reisebürokauffrau
physiotherapist [ˌfɪziə'θerəpɪst]	Physiotherapeut; Physiotherapeutin
plumber ['plʌmə]	Installateur; Installateurin; Klempner; Klempnerin
telephonist [tɪ'lefnɪst]	Telefonist; Telefonistin
bike courier ['baɪk ˌkʊriə]	Fahrradkurier; Fahrradkurierin

p. 16	to **deal with** ['di:l wɪð], **dealt with** ['delt wɪð], **dealt with** ['delt wɪð]	umgehen mit; sich befassen mit; sich kümmern um
	efficient [ɪ'fɪʃnt]	effizient; leistungsfähig
	candidate ['kændɪdət]	Kandidat; Kandidatin; Bewerber; Bewerberin

	experience [ɪk'spɪəriəns]	Erfahrung; Erlebnis
	customer service [ˌkʌstəmə 'sɜ:vɪs]	Kundendienst; Kundenbetreuung
	skill [skɪl]	Kenntnis; Fertigkeit; Fähigkeit
	native speaker [ˌneɪtɪv 'spi:kə]	Muttersprachler; Muttersprachlerin
	certificate [sə'tɪfɪkət]	Zertifikat; Bescheinigung; Urkunde; Zeugnis
	to **offer** ['ɒfə]	bieten; anbieten
	salary ['sælri]	Gehalt
	training ['treɪnɪŋ]	Ausbildung
	CV (= curriculum vitae) [ˌsi:'vi:]	Lebenslauf
	letter of application [ˌletər‿əv‿æplɪ'keɪʃn]	Bewerbungsbrief
	personal statement [ˌpɜ:snl 'steɪtmənt]	Motivationsschreiben
	work experience ['wɜ:k‿ɪkˌspɪəriəns]	Praktikum; Berufserfahrung
	interest ['ɪntrəst]	Interesse
	reference ['refrns]	Referenz; Referenzschreiben
	permanent ['pɜ:mnənt]	unbefristet; permanent; dauerhaft
	communication [kəˌmju:nɪ'keɪʃn]	Kommunikation
	excellent ['ekslnt]	exzellent; hervorragend
	attached [ə'tætʃt]	angefügt; angehängt
	Yours sincerely, [ˌjɔ:z sɪn'sɪəli]	Mit freundlichen Grüßen
p. 17	**preschool** ['pri:sku:l]	Vorschule; Vorschul-
	call centre ['kɔ:l ˌsentə]	Callcenter
	to **pay attention** [ˌpeɪ‿ə'tenʃn]	beachten; aufpassen
	detail ['di:teɪl]	Detail; Einzelheit
	punctual ['pʌŋktʃuəl]	pünktlich
	motivated ['məʊtɪveɪtɪd]	motiviert
p. 18	**such** [sʌtʃ]	solch; solche
p. 19	**Chinese** [tʃaɪ'ni:z]	chinesisch; Chinesisch; aus China; Chinese; Chinesin
	of all the people [əv‿'ɔ:l ðə ˌpi:pl]	von allen Leuten

Reading corner

p. 20	**danger** ['deɪndʒə]	Gefahr
	wonder ['wʌndə]	Wunder
	underwater [ˌʌndə'wɔːtə]	Unterwasser-
	reef [riːf]	Riff
	Sicily ['sɪsɪli]	Sizilien
	moon [muːn]	Mond
	ecosystem ['iːkəʊˌsɪstəm]	Ökosystem
	coral ['kɒrəl]	Koralle
	turtle ['tɜːtl]	Schildkröte
	uncertain [ʌn'sɜːtn]	ungewiss; unsicher
	climate change ['klaɪmət ˌtʃeɪndʒ]	Klimawandel
	bleaching ['bliːtʃɪŋ]	Bleichen; Ausbleichen
	threat [θret]	Bedrohung; Gefahr
	temperature ['temprətʃə]	Temperatur
	changing ['tʃeɪndʒɪŋ]	wechselnd; sich verändernd
	alga *(sg)* ['ælgə], **algae** *(pl)* ['ældʒiː]	Alge
p. 21	**unfortunately** [ʌn'fɔːtʃnətli]	leider; unglücklicherweise
	to **damage** ['dæmɪdʒ]	beschädigen; schaden
	environment [ɪn'vaɪrnmənt]	Umgebung; Umwelt
	snorkelling ['snɔːklɪŋ]	Schnorcheln
	platform ['plætfɔːm]	Plattform
	waste [weɪst]	Abfall; *hier:* Exkremente
	to **pollute** [pə'luːt]	verschmutzen; verunreinigen
	oil spill ['ɔɪl ˌspɪl]	Ölteppich
	destination [ˌdestɪ'neɪʃn]	Ziel; Reiseziel
	to **recover** [rɪ'kʌvə]	sich erholen
	chemical ['kemɪkl]	Chemikalie
	to **stop** [stɒp]	aufhalten; stoppen
	scientist ['saɪəntɪst]	Wissenschaftler; Wissenschaftlerin
	extinct [ɪk'stɪŋkt]	ausgestorben
	to **care (about sth)** ['keər (əˌbaʊt)]	(etw.) wichtig nehmen; sich interessieren (für etw.)

Film corner

. 23	**whale shark** ['weɪl ˌʃɑ:k]	Walhai
	saltwater crocodile [sɔ:ltˌwɔ:tə 'krɒkədaɪl]	Salzwasserkrokodil
	manta ray ['mæntə‿reɪ]	Teufelsrochen
	close [kləʊs]	eng; nahe
	up to ['ʌp tə]	bis zu

1 Write the words and find an area in Australia.

1. Australia is one of the largest countries in the world, and it is the only country that is also a ☐ _ _ _ _ _ _ _ _ _.
2. A person from Australia is an ☐ _ _ _ _ _ _ _ _ _.
3. Aboriginal people still ☐ _ _ _ _ _ _ for their rights in Australia.
4. ☐ _ _ _ _ _ _ _ _ _ people have been in Australia for over 50,000 years.
5. Australians love sport, parties and the beach. They are very ☐ _ _ - _ _ _ _ _.
6. About 30 million years ago Australia broke away from _ _ _ _ _ ☐ _ _ _ _.
7. There are some unusual animals, like the ☐ _ _ _ _, that can only be found in Australia.

The huge area in the centre of Australia is called the '_ _ _ _ _ _ _'.

2 What can you see in the pictures?

1.  ______________________

2.  ______________________

3.  ______________________

4.  ______________________

5.  ______________________

3 Complete the text.

Koa: Good morning everyone. My name is Koa and I'm your t_ _ _ _ _ _ _ _ today. I'm going to s_ _ _ you a_ _ _ _ _ Uluru.

Uluru is s_ _ _ _ _ _ to us. In fact, each part of the landscape has a special m_ _ _ _ _ _. We believe that giant c_ _ _ _ _ _ _ _ came and made the mountains, rocks and rivers a long time ago. We call that time 'Dreamtime'.

Our culture may seem difficult to understand to other p_ _ _ _ _. But we have to protect places like Uluru and the people who visit them, so we have special rules for visitors. Visitors are not allowed to c_ _ _ _ Uluru, so we are going to walk around the rock today. Please stay on the p_ _ _ and don't throw your rubbish on the earth, OK? If you're ready, let's go!

4 Write the words in English and German.

1.  ______________ ______________

2. 

______________ ______________

3.  ______________ ______________

4.  ______________ ______________

5 Complete the text.

applicationCVdestinationletterreferencessendingskillsexperience

INTERNET

Working in Australia

With 240 sunny days a year, Australia is a popular ______________ for people who are looking for a new place to live and work. People who have ________ that Australia needs will find it easier to get a job.

Finding a job

The best way to find a job is to look at job ads. Ads have information about the job and about the work ______________ and the skills that are needed to do it.

Applying for a job

When you ________ ______ your______________,
you usually have to include:

– a ______________ of application,

– a __________ with a personal statement,

– ______________ from other jobs you have had.

6 Find the words and complete the e-mail.

angehängt | effizient | Fertigkeiten | Kommunikation | motiviert | Muttersprachler | sich freuen auf | Zertifikat | Referenzen | hervorragend | Erfahrung

MAIL

Dear Mrs Davis,

I would like to apply for the job as tour guide at Uluru-Kata Tjuta National Park. Last year I did a tour guide course in Alice Springs and I have a ________________.

You can see in my ________________ that I am reliable, ________________ and very ________________.

Although I am only 18 years old, I already have some ________________. My parents have a B&B and I help them at weekends. Our guests come from all over the world and I enjoy talking to them and telling them about Australia.

I am a ________________ ________________ of English.

I have strong ________________ skills and ________________ computer ________________.

Please find ________________ my CV.

I __________ ______________ ______ hearing from you.

Yours sincerely,

Koa Walker

7 Complete the dialogue.

Dana: Hi Amy. How was your interview?

Amy: It was OK. I think my s_ _ _ _ _ make me a good c_ _ _ _ _ _ _ _ for the job. I just hope Mr Pitt thinks so too.

Dana: Why wouldn't he? You have great c_ _ _ _ _ _ _ _ _ _ _ _ skills, you're m_ _ _ _ _ _ _ _ and always p_ _ _ _ _ _ _.

Amy: I hope I'm the person with the most experience that they have interviewed. It would be wonderful to have p_ _ _ _ _ _ _ _ work.

Dana: What about the s_ _ _ _ _?

Amy: It's one of the largest hotels in Melbourne, so the salary is good and they offer t_ _ _ _ _ _ _.

Dana: That's great, Amy. I really hope you get the job!

Amy: Thanks, Dana. Me too.

8 Match the verbs and complete the sentences.

a) Match the verbs and write the German.

1. be	a) able to	______________
2. care	b) with	______________
3. look	c) attention to	______________
4. pay	d) forward to	______________
5. deal	e) about	______________

b) Complete the sentences with words from a).

1. As a tour guide it is important to be able to _ _ _ _ _ _ _ _ all kinds of people.
2. If you are someone who can _ _ _ _ _ _ _ _ _ _ _ _ _ _ _ _ detail, you'll be a good tour guide.
3. After the course you'll _ _ _ _ _ _ _ _ answer tourists' questions.
4. I _ _ _ _ _ _ _ _ _ _ _ _ _ _ _ working as a tour guide.
5. I want to teach tourists to _ _ _ _ _ _ _ _ _ Uluru and our culture.

9 Find the words and complete the text.

greatestmoonreefsSicilyunderwaterwonders

INTERNET

The Great Barrier Reef is one of the ____________ ____________ in the world. It is an amazing ____________ world with thousands of ____________ and hundreds of islands. It is 2,300 kilometres long, which is about the distance from ____________ to London. It is larger than the Great Wall of China and you can even see it from the ____________!

10 Write the words in English and German.

1.  ____________ ____________

2.  ____________ ____________

3.  ____________ ____________

4.  ____________ ____________

11 Find the words and complete the text.

Chemikalien | Gefahr | Klimawandel
Koralle | Lebewesen | schaden
sich erholen | Temperaturen | verschmutzen

INTERNET

Save our reef!

The Great Barrier Reef is home to more than 350 types of ______________ and hundreds of different fish and birds. It's a very special place but it is in ______________. If we don't protect this underwater wonder, it could disappear forever.

______________ ______________ and higher ______________ in the water are big problems. When the water in the sea gets hotter, algae die and the corals lose their beautiful colours.

A lot of animals need algae for food. So, when algae die, many sea ______________ die too. Chemicals are also a problem. Rain washes ______________ from farms into rivers and the rivers carry them to the sea. The chemicals ______________ the sea and ______________ plants and animals.

The Great Barrier Reef can ______________, but we must save it now!

12 What can you see in the pictures?

1.  ______________________

2.  ______________________

3.  ______________________

4.  ______________________

13 Find 8 verbs.

E	M	I	G	R	A	T	E	T	M
X	U	Z	A	O	D	E	G	A	S
P	E	B	T	R	P	Y	D	K	T
L	Q	Z	S	V	I	S	S	E	R
O	F	F	E	R	S	T	C	O	U
R	I	U	N	J	T	O	W	F	G
E	R	V	D	H	W	P	M	F	G
U	E	B	I	A	K	S	P	N	L
C	O	M	N	B	E	H	A	V	E

1. auswandern ______________________
2. kämpfen; sich anstrengen ______________________
3. erkunden; erforschen ______________________
4. bieten; anbieten ______________________
5. sich benehmen; sich verhalten ______________________
6. einschicken; einsenden ______________________
7. abnehmen; ausziehen ______________________
8. aufhalten; stoppen ______________________

14 Find the words.

▼ 1. a school where you learn and live
3. travel to an area or a country to learn about it
4. She has the experience and skills that are … for the job.
6. The … killed thousands of Aboriginal people.
8. not many

▶ 2. the group of people who are responsible for a country
5. I'm so sorry! I didn't … that it was so late.
7. a rule
9. The birds' … washes into the sea.
10. Many Australian cities are … to the coast.

15 Find the words and complete the dialogue.

chingblea | ticnext | sicsistent | galea | meetsocys | hatter

Jamie: How was your trip to the Great Barrier Reef?

Frida: It was really interesting, thanks. I didn't realise just how huge it is or what an amazing ________________ it is. Did you know it is home to more than 350 types of coral?

Jamie: Seriously? Wow! I didn't know that.

Frida: But the trip made me sad too. The coral is losing its beautiful colours.

Jamie: It's because of coral ________________, isn't it?

Frida: Yes. When the water gets warmer, this kills the ________________ on the coral and it loses its colour.

Jamie: I read that another ________________ is the chemicals that pollute the sea.

Frida: Yes, the tour guide told us that rain washes chemicals from farms into the sea. And that ________________ say the reef may be ________________ by 2030 if we don't find a solution.

Jamie: That would be so sad! The governments of the world have to find a plan to stop climate change.

●16 Complete the sentences with the words.

1. **Vorschule** My mum is a ______________ teacher. She teaches children from ages 3 to 6.
2. **Callcenter** My sister works in a __________ ______________. She is on the phone all day.
3. **ungewiss** The future of the Great Barrier Reef is ______________________.
4. **solch; solche** Australia is _____________ an amazing country.
5. **von allen** Of _______ _______ ____________ I know, my sister is the most motivated.

Unit 2 Colourful Caribbean

p. 28	**the Caribbean** [ðə ˌkærɪ'bi:ən]	die Karibik

Way in

p. 28	**tropical** ['trɒpɪkl]	tropisch
	autumn ['ɔ:təm]	Herbst
	hurricane ['hʌrɪkən]	Orkan; Wirbelsturm
	tourist industry ['tʊərɪst‿ɪndəstri]	Tourismus
p. 29	**Caribbean** [ˌkærɪ'bi:ən]	karibisch; Karibisch; Karibe; Karibin
	French [frenʃ]	französisch; aus Frankreich
	Dutch [dʌtʃ]	niederländisch; Niederländisch
	descendant [dɪ'sendənt]	Abkömmling; Nachfahre; Nachfahrin
	rhythm ['rɪðm]	Rhythmus
	at first [ət 'fɜ:st]	zuerst; zunächst
	the British [ðə 'brɪtɪʃ]	die Briten
	South America [ˌsaʊθ‿ə'merɪkə]	Südamerika
p. 28	**Jamaican** [dʒə'meɪkən]	Jamaikaner; Jamaikanerin
p. 29	**role model** ['rəʊl ˌmɒdl]	Vorbild
	lyrics *(pl)* ['lɪrɪks]	Liedtext
	return [rɪ'tɜ:n]	Rückkehr
	full-time [ˌfʊl'taɪm]	Vollzeit-; Ganztags-
	musician [mju:'zɪʃn]	Musiker; Musikerin
	goal [gəʊl]	Ziel; Tor

Station 1

Holiday words

ferry ['feri]	Fähre
sand [sænd]	Sand
sunshine ['sʌnʃaɪn]	Sonnenschein

accommodation [əˌkɒmə'deɪʃn]	Unterbringung; Unterkunft
passport ['pɑːspɔːt]	Pass; Reisepass
departure [dɪ'pɑːtʃə]	Abflug; Abreise
arrival [ə'raɪvl]	Ankunft
to **board** [bɔːd]	an Bord gehen
suitcase ['suːtkeɪs]	Koffer
check-in ['tʃekɪn]	Gepäckaufgabe; Einchecken
couch surfing ['kaʊtʃ ˌsɜːfɪŋ]	Couchsurfing
luggage ['lʌgɪdʒ]	Gepäck
breeze [briːz]	Brise
luxury ['lʌkʃri]	Luxus; Luxus-
delay [dɪ'leɪ]	Verzögerung; Verspätung
gate [geɪt]	Gate; Ausgang
diving ['daɪvɪŋ]	Tauchen; Tauch-

p. 30	**hopping** ['hɒpɪŋ]	Hüpfen; Hopping
	the Bahamas [ðə bə'hɑːməz]	die Bahamas *(Inselgruppe in der Karibik)*
	simply ['sɪmpli]	einfach nur
	nearby [ˌnɪə'baɪ]	in der Nähe
	distant ['dɪstnt]	entfernt; distanziert
	beauty ['bjuːti]	Schönheit
	to **take one's breath away** [ˌteɪk wʌnz 'breθ‿əˌweɪ]	den Atem rauben
	to **dive** [daɪv]	tauchen
	to **discover** [dɪ'skʌvə]	entdecken
	beginner [bɪ'gɪnə]	Anfänger; Anfängerin
	shipwreck ['ʃɪprek]	Schiffswrack
	Trinidad ['trɪnɪdæd]	Trinidad *(Insel in der Karibik)*
	steelpan ['stiːlpæn]	Steelpan *(Trommel aus Blech)*
	seafood ['siːfuːd]	Meeresfrüchte
	nature ['neɪtʃə]	Natur

	volcano *(sg)* [vɒl'keɪnəʊ], **volcanoes** *(pl)* [vɒl'keɪnəʊz]	Vulkan
	extraordinary [ɪk'strɔ:dnri]	außergewöhnlich
p. 31	**mist** [mɪst]	Nebel; Dunst

Station 2

Standards and values

complicated ['kɒmplɪkeɪtɪd]	kompliziert
to **marry** ['mæri]	heiraten
friendship ['frendʃɪp]	Freundschaft
religion [rɪ'lɪdʒn]	Religion
disadvantaged [ˌdɪsəd'vɑ:ntɪdʒd]	benachteiligt
fair [feə]	gerecht; fair
values *(pl)* ['vælju:z]	Werte; Wertvorstellungen
well-paid [ˌwel'peɪd]	gut bezahlt
commitment [kə'mɪtmənt]	Engagement; Einsatz
honesty ['ɒnɪsti]	Ehrlichkeit
responsibility [rɪˌspɒnsə'bɪləti]	Verantwortung
solidarity [ˌsɒlɪ'dærəti]	Solidarität

p. 34	**last night** [ˌlɑ:st 'naɪt]	gestern Abend; gestern Nacht
	nursing ['nɜ:sɪŋ]	Pflege; Krankenpflege
	violence *(no pl)* ['vaɪələns]	Gewalt
	shooting ['ʃu:tɪŋ]	Schießerei
	drug [drʌg]	Droge
	to **keep** [ki:p]	*hier:* bleiben
	to **let** [let], **let** [let], **let** [let]	lassen
	whether ['weðə]	ob
	to **be involved** [bi: ɪn'vɒlvd]	sich beteiligen; sich engagieren
	counsellor ['kaʊnslə]	Berater; Beraterin

	to **wonder** ['wʌndə]	sich Gedanken machen; sich fragen
	fee [fiː]	Gebühr
	to **come out** [kʌm‿'aʊt]	sich outen
	gay [geɪ]	schwul; homosexuell
	shock [ʃɒk]	Schock
	on the one hand [ɒn ðə‿'wʌn ˌhænd]	einerseits
	on the other hand [ɒn ði‿'ʌðə ˌhænd]	andererseits
p. 37	to **grow** [grəʊ]	ansteigen
	to **feed** [fiːd]	ernähren
	to **shoot** [ʃuːt], **shot** [ʃɒt], **shot** [ʃɒt]	erschießen
	statement ['steɪtmənt]	Aussage; Behauptung
	furthermore [ˌfɜːðə'mɔː]	überdies; außerdem

Reading corner

p. 38	to **lie** [laɪ], **lay** [leɪ], **lain** [leɪn]	liegen
	position [pə'zɪʃn]	Position; Stelle
	governess ['gʌvnəs]	Gouvernante; Hauslehrerin
	Barbados [bɑː'beɪdɒs]	Barbados *(Inselstaat in der Karibik)*
p. 39	**terrifying** ['terəfaɪɪŋ]	schrecklich; fürchterlich
	peaceful ['piːsfl]	friedlich
	porthole ['pɔːthəʊl]	Bullauge; Luke
	cabin ['kæbɪn]	Kabine
	brutal ['bruːtl]	brutal
	at that time [ət ðæt 'taɪm]	damals; zu der Zeit
	perhaps [pə'hæps]	vielleicht
	to **fly open** [ˌflaɪ‿'əʊpn]	auffliegen
	to **recognise** ['rekəgnaɪz]	erkennen
	evil ['iːvl]	böse; schlecht
	look [lʊk]	Ausdruck; Blick
	ugly ['ʌgli]	hässlich
	to **open** ['əʊpn]	sich öffnen; aufgehen
	horror ['hɒrə]	Horror; Schrecken; Entsetzen

p. 40	**punishment** ['pʌnɪʃmənt]	Bestrafung
	dagger ['dægə]	Dolch
	to **walk the plank** [ˌwɔ:k ðə 'plæŋk]	über eine Schiffsplanke ins Wasser getrieben werden
	smile [smaɪl]	Lächeln
	to **continue** [kən'tɪnju:]	fortfahren; weitergehen
	to **think of** ['θɪŋk‿əv]	sich ausdenken; sich einfallen lassen
	to **fool sb** [fu:l]	jmdn. täuschen
	prisoner ['prɪznə]	Gefangener; Gefangene
	to **cry** [kraɪ]	weinen; schreien; rufen
	to **be terrified (of sth)** [bi: 'terəfaɪd (əv)]	(große) Angst (vor etw.) haben
p. 41	**sky** [skaɪ]	Himmel
	shout [ʃaʊt]	Ruf
	to **hunt** [hʌnt]	jagen
	to **fire** [faɪə]	schießen mit; abfeuern
	obviously ['ɒbviəsli]	offensichtlich
	to **stop** [stɒp]	stehen bleiben; anhalten
	to **get away (from sb)** [ˌget‿ə'weɪ frəm]	(jmdm.) entkommen; (von jmdm.) wegkommen

Film corner

p. 43	**season** ['si:zn]	Jahreszeit; Saison
	dry [draɪ]	trocken
	heat [hi:t]	Hitze

1 Write the words and find an adjective.

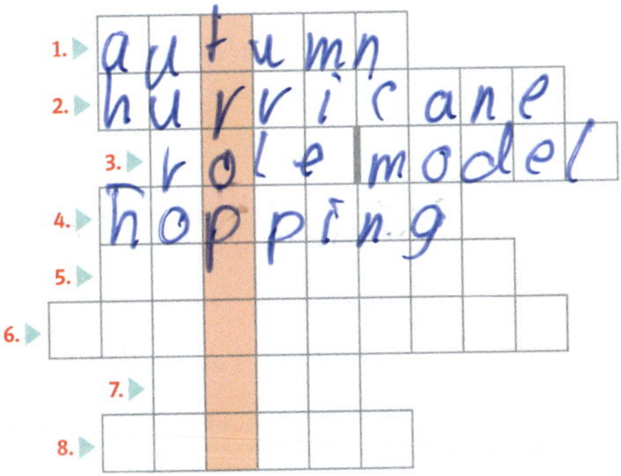

1. the season that comes after summer
2. a very strong wind
3. Bob Marley is a … for many musicians.
4. Island … is a good way to discover the Caribbean.
5. an island in the Caribbean
6. the child and the child's child of a person
7. The beaches have beautiful white … .
8. Jamaica was a British … from 1707 until 1962.

The Caribbean has a … climate.

2 What can you see in the pictures?

1.  shipwreck
2. 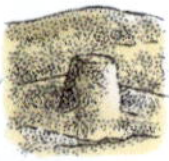 Sand
3.  seafood
4.  ____________

3 Find 5 islands.

1. the B_ _ _ _ _ _
2. C_ _ _
3. J_ _ _ _ _ _
4. B_ _ _ _ _ _ _
5. T_ _ _ _ _ _ _

4 Write the words in English and German.

1.  ____________ ____________
2.  ____________ ____________
3.  ____________ ____________
4.  ____________ ____________

5 Find the words and complete the dialogue.

Dylan: Bob, you've been to ________ ____________. What's it like?

Bob: It's amazing! The beaches have white ________ and the sea is warm and blue. Their ____________ takes your ________ ________!

Dylan: Were most of the Caribbean islands colonies?

Bob: Yes. I've only visited Jamaica, which was an English ____________. Nearly ______ ______ people there are ____________ of slaves who were brought there from Africa. A lot of people work in the ____________ ____________, but a lot are unemployed.

Dylan: That's what I heard. It looks like paradise – but it's not for the people who live there.

6 Complete the text.

beginner | discover | dive | extraordinary | hopping | last night | party | terrified | seafood | shipwreck

BLOG

My Caribbean dream

After island __________ in the Bahamas for a few days, I decided to take a flight to Barbados next. I arrived yesterday, ready to __________ dolphins, turtles and all the other __________ sea life.

I can't believe how beautiful it is here – I love my life!

______ __________ I visited the diving school where I learned how to ______ when I was a __________.

The instructors are all very friendly and so much fun! One of the instructors is from Trinidad.

He told me that people really know how to ______ there and that the __________ is amazing.

I think I'll go there next! Anyway, the instructors invited me to dive to a __________ tomorrow.

I'm so excited! And a bit __________.

7 Match the verbs and complete the sentences.

a) Match the verbs and write the German.

1. be involved	a) out	______________________
2. get	b) of	______________________
3. come	c) in	______________________
4. think	d) place	______________________
5. take	e) away	______________________

b) Complete the sentences with words from a).

1. Eliza knew how she could _ _ _ _   _ _ _ _ from the pirates.
2. The carnival in Trinidad _ _ _ _ _   _ _ _ _ _ every February.
3. Blackheart liked to _ _ _ _ _   _ _ special punishments for his men.
4. Tara is _ _ _ _ _ _ _ _   _ _ helping teenagers in her community.
5. My cousin _ _ _ _   _ _ _ as gay last week. We're all really happy for him.

8 Complete the table.

Infinitive	Simple past	Present perfect (has/have ...)
1. cry	______	______
2. feed	______	______
3. ______	flew open	______
4. grow	______	______
5. let	______	______
6. ______	______	lain
7. ______	thought of	______

9 Write the words in English and German.

1.  ______ ______

2.  ______ ______

3.  ______ ______

4.  ______ ______

10 Find the words and complete the text.

Beraterin | Gewalt | Schießereien | engagiert in | Drogen | überall | Krankenpflege | stark bleiben

Teacher: Hello, Tara. Thank you for talking to me today about studying ________________ at Ontario College, here in Canada. First, could you tell me why you want to do the course?

Tara: Yes, of course. Well, as you know, I live in Kingston in a very poor area. ____________ are sold ____________________.
________________ breaks out regularly and there are __________________ nearly every day.
I will be so happy to get out of here.

Teacher: Living there must be very hard for you.

Tara: Yes, but my family helps me to __________ ____________. I am also a __________________ at my church. I love helping people, which is why I want to become a nurse.

Teacher: So you're really ________________ ________ your community. That's great, but won't you miss your family when you move here?

Tara: Yes, but we will be able to talk every day, thanks to the internet!

11 Find the words.

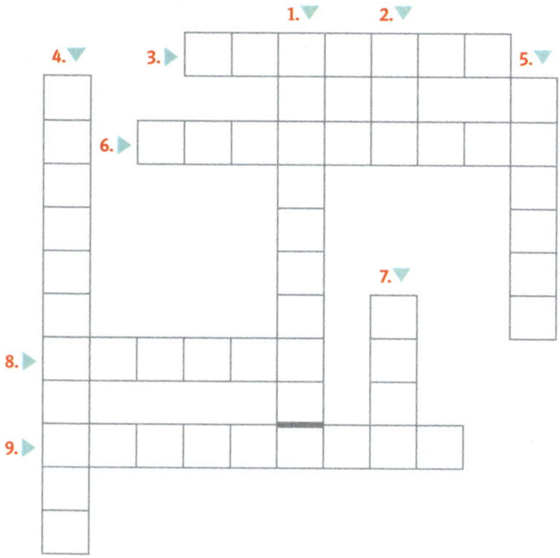

▼ 1. Read the … and decide whether it is right or wrong.
2. Seeming confident in an interview is quite an … .
4. …, I agree with your reasons.
5. not far away
7. It's my … to be the best in the team.

▶ 3. far away in space or time
6. the time when a train or plane leaves a certain place
8. come back to a place
9. With all the guns around, it's … not a safe place to live.

12 Find the words and complete the text.

INTERNET

Captain Blackheart

In the 17th century the Caribbean Sea was a very dangerous place. Pirate attacks on Spanish colonies and ships ____________ ____________ all the time. One of the most famous pirates at ____________ ____________ was the ________________ Captain Blackheart. He was a tall man with black hair, black eyes, yellow teeth – and an ____________ ____________.

He looked awful and everyone was ________________ ________ him. Blackheart loved two things: gold, and thinking of special ____________________ for his ____________________, and any man on board who tried to fight him.

Captain Blackheart was afraid of only one thing: the HMS Revenge, a Royal Navy ship that ________________ pirates.

13 Find 8 verbs.

C	A	U	C	O	N	T	I	N	U	E
R	I	R	E	P	C	H	M	S	S	J
Y	O	T	T	E	X	R	E	W	A	M
O	C	W	O	N	D	E	R	O	V	W
U	A	R	X	V	V	C	O	N	E	R
R	E	C	O	G	N	I	S	E	B	E
A	K	A	S	A	C	R	U	E	U	G
G	E	T	A	W	A	Y	F	R	O	M
E	T	E	E	A	S	E	I	C	D	E
V	O	N	G	Y	E	M	R	Y	X	T
P	D	I	S	C	O	V	E	R	E	O

1. fortfahren ____________________
2. weinen ____________________
3. entdecken ____________________
4. abfeuern ____________________
5. entkommen ____________________
6. sich öffnen ____________________
7. erkennen ____________________
8. sich Gedanken machen ____________________

14 Find the words and complete the dialogue.

binca | folo | klaw teh pankl | vile | nessgrove | ragged | toosh

Mark: Have you read *Eliza's Voyage* yet?

Sarah: Yes, I loved it! What did you think of it?

Mark: I thought it was really exciting. What was your favourite part?

Sarah: That's easy. It's when the pirate follows Carol and Eliza into the ________________ with such an ____________ look. Eliza pushes him away, but then Blackheart walks in, with his ______________ in his hand.

Mark: I liked that part too! Then Blackheart says that Eliza will ____________ _______ ______________, but of course he didn't know she was a ___ ___________ because she was wearing men's clothes.

Sarah: And she didn't say anything! She didn't want the pirates to know that she had tried to ____________ them.

Mark: Of course not. She was so brave!

Sarah: And she was lucky! Lucky that they didn't ______________ her!

Unit 3 Around South Africa

p. 48	**South Africa** [ˌsaʊθ‿ˈæfrɪkə]	Südafrika

Way in

p. 48	**main** [meɪn]	Haupt-
	amount (of) [əˈmaʊnt (əv)]	Menge; Summe
	diamond [ˈdaɪəmənd]	Diamant
	safari [səˈfɑːri]	Safari
	lion [ˈlaɪən]	Löwe
	rhino [ˈraɪnəʊ]	Rhinozeros; Nashorn
	national park [ˌnæʃnl ˈpɑːk]	Nationalpark
	nature reserve [ˈneɪtʃə rɪˌzɜːv]	Naturschutzgebiet
p. 49	**South African** [ˌsaʊθ‿ˈæfrɪkən]	Südafrikaner; Südafrikanerin
	media [ˈmiːdiə]	Medien
	the Dutch [ðə ˈdʌtʃ]	die Niederländer
	apartheid *(no pl)* [əˈpɑːtaɪt]	Apartheid *(Rassentrennung per Gesetz)*
	to **separate** [ˈsepreɪt]	trennen
	to **build** [bɪld]	*hier:* gründen
	nation [ˈneɪʃn]	Nation; Land; Staat
	gated community [ˌgeɪtɪd kəˈmjuːnəti]	bewachte Wohnanlage; geschlossene Wohnanlage
	township [ˈtaʊnʃɪp]	Township *(Wohnsiedlungen für Schwarze in Südafrika)*
	to **migrate** [maɪˈgreɪt]	ziehen; wandern
	territory [ˈterɪtri]	Gebiet; Revier; Territorium
	war [wɔː]	Krieg
	democratic [ˌdeməˈkrætɪk]	demokratisch
	election [ɪˈlekʃn]	Wahl
	constitution [kɒnstɪˈtjuːʃn]	Verfassung

Station 1

Social differences

consequence ['kɒnsɪkwəns]	Konsequenz; Folge; Auswirkung
victim ['vɪktɪm]	Opfer
to **drop out of** [ˌdrɒp‿'aʊt‿əv]	abbrechen
health insurance ['helθ‿ɪnˌʃʊərns]	Krankenversicherung
well-educated [ˌwel'edʒʊkeɪtɪd]	gut ausgebildet
state school ['steɪt ˌsku:l]	staatliche Schule; öffentliche Schule
the rich [ðə 'rɪtʃ]	die Reichen
to **be middle class** [bi: ˌmɪdl 'klɑ:s]	zur Mittelschicht gehören
privileged ['prɪvlɪdʒd]	privilegiert; bevorzugt
equal ['i:kwəl]	gleich; gleichberechtigt
unfairness [ʌn'feənəs]	Ungerechtigkeit
privilege ['prɪvlɪdʒ]	Privileg; (Vor-)Recht
equality [ɪ'kwɒləti]	Gleichberechtigung; Ebenbürtigkeit

p. 50	**face** [feɪs]	Gesicht
	injury ['ɪndʒri]	Verletzung
	to **suffer** ['sʌfə]	leiden; erleiden
	crash [kræʃ]	Zusammenstoß
	Dear Sir or Madam, [dɪə ˌsɜ:r‿ɔ: 'mædəm]	Sehr geehrte Damen und Herren,
	Yours faithfully, [ˌjɔ:z 'feɪθfli]	Mit freundlichen Grüßen
	to **go on** [ˌgəʊ‿'ɒn]	weitermachen; weitergehen
	further ['fɜ:ðə]	weiter
	questioning ['kwestʃənɪŋ]	Verhör; Vernehmung

	construction [kən'strʌkʃn]	Bau; Konstruktion; Aufbau
	to **show up** [ˌʃəʊ‿'ʌp]	auftauchen; erscheinen
p. 51	**health** [helθ]	Gesundheit
	nightmare ['naɪtmeə]	Albtraum
	guard [gɑːd]	Wache; Wächter; Wächterin
	someone stupid [ˌsʌmwʌn 'stjuːpɪd]	irgendein Idiot
	fault [fɔːlt]	Schuld
	guilty ['gɪlti]	schuldig
	treatment ['triːtmənt]	Behandlung
p. 52	**opposite** ['ɒpəzɪt]	Gegenteil

Station 2

Landscapes

wide [waɪd]	groß; breit; weit; ausgedehnt
endless ['endləs]	endlos
plain [pleɪn]	Ebene
flat [flæt]	flach; platt
fence [fens]	Zaun
mountain range ['maʊntɪn ˌreɪndʒ]	Bergkette; Gebirge
marsh [mɑːʃ]	Sumpf; Moor
pond [pɒnd]	Teich; Tümpel
spring [sprɪŋ]	Quelle
canal [kə'næl]	Kanal
valley ['væli]	Tal

p. 54	**ranger** *(AE)* ['reɪndʒə]	Ranger; Rangerin
	to **name** [neɪm]	nennen; benennen
	tourism ['tʊərɪzm]	Tourismus
	success [sək'ses]	Erfolg

	ever since [ˌevə 'sɪns]	seitdem
	to **conserve** [kən'sɜːv]	erhalten; bewahren
	ivory ['aɪvri]	Elfenbein
	to **face** [feɪs]	gegenüberstehen; konfrontiert werden mit
	challenge ['tʃælɪndʒ]	Herausforderung
	to **regulate** ['regjəleɪt]	vorschreiben; bestimmen; regeln
	to **reduce** [rɪ'djuːs]	reduzieren; vermindern; verringern
	to **recycle** [ˌriː'saɪkl]	recyceln; wiederverwerten
	leopard ['lepəd]	Leopard; Leopardin
	buffalo *(sg)* ['bʌfləʊ], **buffaloes** *(pl)* ['bʌfləʊz]	Büffel
	game [geɪm]	Wild
	hunter ['hʌntə]	Jäger; Jägerin
	to **treat** [triːt]	behandeln
	to **deserve** [dɪ'zɜːv]	verdienen
	poaching ['pəʊtʃɪŋ]	Wilderei; Wildern
	up [ʌp]	abgelaufen
	chatroom ['tʃætrʊm]	Chatroom
p. 55	to **go on** [ˌgəʊ‿'ɒn]	geschehen; passieren
	to **protest** [prə'test]	protestieren
	baby elephant ['beɪbi ˌelɪfənt]	Elefantenbaby
	to **suggest** [sə'dʒest]	vorschlagen; nahelegen; andeuten
p. 56	to **leave** [liːv]	zurücklassen; vergessen

Reading corner

p. 58	**alive** [ə'laɪv]	belebt
	to **skip** [skɪp]	hüpfen; springen; überspringen
	bench [benʃ]	Bank; Sitzbank
	rough [rʌf]	rau; grob; derb
	primary school ['praɪmri ˌskuːl]	Grundschule
	to **take turns** [ˌteɪk 'tɜːnz]	sich abwechseln
	classmate ['klɑːsmeɪt]	Mitschüler; Mitschülerin

	cactus ['kæktəs]	Kaktus
	sprinkler ['sprɪŋklə]	Rasensprenger
	to **sweep (up)** [swi:p (ʌp)], **swept (up)** [swept (ʌp)], **swept (up)** [swept (ʌp)]	(hoch)heben; (auf)fegen
	bottom ['bɒtəm]	Hintern; Po
	savage ['sævɪdʒ]	Wilder; Wilde
	to **lead** [li:d], **led** [led], **led** [led]	führen; anführen; leiten
p. 59	**grey-haired** [ˌgreɪ'heəd]	grauhaarig
	to **pray** [preɪ]	beten
	playing field ['pleɪɪŋ ˌfi:ld]	Sportplatz
	New Year [ˌnju: 'jɪə]	Neujahr
	to **stare** [steə]	starren
p. 60	**protester** [prə'testə]	Demonstrant; Demonstrantin
	black (person) [blæk]	Schwarzer; Schwarze
	headteacher [ˌhed'ti:tʃə]	Schulleiter; Schulleiterin
	to **stop sb from sth** ['stɒp frəm]	jmdn. von etw. abhalten; jmdn. an etw. hindern
	to **enter** ['entə]	hineingehen; betreten; eintreten
	anyone ['eniwʌn]	irgendjemand *(in Fragesätzen)*
	to **pick** [pɪk]	pflücken
	to **leave sb alone** [ˌli:v‿ə'ləʊn]	jmdn. in Ruhe lassen
	to **turn around** [ˌtɜ:n‿ə'raʊnd]	(sich) umdrehen; wenden
	atmosphere ['ætməsfɪə]	Atmosphäre; Stimmung
	to **turn to sb** ['tɜ:n tə]	sich jmdm. zuwenden
	to **pause** [pɔ:z]	(eine kurze) Pause machen; innehalten
	awkward ['ɔ:kwəd]	ungünstig; ungeschickt; unbeholfen; peinlich
	to **go red** [ˌgəʊ 'red]	rot werden
	to **shake one's head** [ˌʃeɪk wʌns 'hed]	den Kopf schütteln

	one step at a time [ˌwʌn stepˬætˬə ˈtaɪm]	schrittweise; ein Schritt nach dem anderen
	to **smile** [smaɪl]	lächeln
	to **take a deep breath** [ˌteɪkˬə ˌdiːp ˈbreθ]	tief einatmen; tief Luft holen

Film corner

p. 63	**baboon** [bəˈbuːn]	Pavian
	puppet [ˈpʌpɪt]	Puppe; Handpuppe

1 Write the words and find a capital city.

1. From 1948 to 1994 the system of ☐ _ _ _ _ _ _ _ _ strictly separated black and white people in South Africa.
2. When South Africa became a British colony, the Dutch moved to a new _ _ ☐ _ _ _ _ _ _ .
3. ☐ _ _ _ _ _   _ _ _ _ _ _ _ was president of South Africa from 1994 to 1999.
4. Many rich people live in gated communities, while poor people live in ☐ _ _ _ _ _ _ _ _ .
5. A person from South Africa is a _ ☐ _ _ _ _ _ _ _ _ _ _ _ .
6. A _ _ _ _ ☐ _   _ _ _ _ _ _ _ is an area of land where the animals and plants are protected.
7. South Africa has large amounts of gold and _ ☐ _ _ _ _ _ _ .
8. Kruger _ ☐ _ _ _ _ _ _   _ _ _ _ is one of the best places in the country to see the 'Big Five'.

The president of South Africa has his seat in _ _ _ _ _ _ _ _ .

2 Complete the text.

INTERNET

South Africa is a country of many cultures. Aboriginal people lived in South Africa long before the first European settlers arrived from the Netherlands and Great Britain.

In 1814 the country became a British c_ _ _ _ _ and t_ _ D_ _ _ _ _ settled in Cape Town. On 31 May 1910, eight years after the end of the second Boer w_ _, South Africa won its independence. In 1948 the government introduced 'a_ _ _ _ _ _ _ _', a system which s_ _ _ _ _ _ _ _ black and white people. In 1994, when Nelson Mandela became president after the first d_ _ _ _ _ _ _ _ _ e_ _ _ _ _ _ _ _, apartheid was abolished. Mandela promised to b_ _ _ _ a new 'rainbow n_ _ _ _ _' for all the people of South Africa.

Today many rich people still live in safe and comfortable g_ _ _ _ c_ _ _ _ _ _ _ _ _ _, while poor people live in t_ _ _ _ _ _ _ _, often without clean water or electricity.

3 What can you see in the pictures?

1.  ______________________________
2.  ______________________________
3.  ______________________________
4.  ______________________________

4 Complete the text.

faceinjuriesquestioningsufferedcrashtreatment

Durban News

Today at around 1 p.m. there was an accident between a bus and a car in Durban. The bus was taking students to Redhill School. The bus driver died soon after the ______________. One student was taken to hospital with __________ ______________. The driver of the car ______________ back injuries and was taken to hospital for ______________.

The passenger was not hurt.

A young worker said he saw the car driving towards the bus. The police took the young man to the police station for ______________.

5 Find the words and complete the e-mail.

Albträume | Mit freundlichen Grüßen | schuldig | Sehr geehrte Damen und Herren | Behandlung | Zusammenstoß | weitermachen | Schuld

MAIL

_______ _______ ____ ___________,

I would like to answer the letter from Mr Botha in the *Durban News* on Monday. I am the daughter of the woman who was driving the car that caused the ___________ on 10 January.

I agree with Mr Botha in general, but my mother is not a crazy driver. She had just heard that she had lost her job and probably wasn't concentrating. She feels so ___________ and is struggling with the situation because she thinks it was her ___________.

She often can't sleep and when she does, she has ___________.

My mother really needs to see a doctor for ___________, but we can't afford one. I don't know how we can _______ _______.

_______ ___________,

Cebile Sekibo

6 Write the words in English and German.

1.  ____________ ____________
2.  ____________ ____________
3.  ____________ ____________
4.  ____________ ____________
5.  ____________ ____________

7 Complete the text.

Kruger National Park

Opened in 1926, Kruger National Park was South Africa's first national park. The goal of the park is to protect and c_ _ _ _ _ _ _ South African wildlife. Tourists can see the 'Big Five' in the park – the name given by big g_ _ _ hunters to the elephant, lion, rhino, l_ _ _ _ _ _ and b_ _ _ _ _ _. These animals are also the most dangerous, which is why the r_ _ _ _ _ _ treat them with the respect they d_ _ _ _ _ _. Before the park was founded, animals were hunted and many elephants were killed for their i_ _ _ _. The rangers still f_ _ _ lots of c_ _ _ _ _ _ _ _ _ today and are trying hard to r_ _ _ _ _ the amount of p_ _ _ _ _ _ _ too.

8 Find the words.

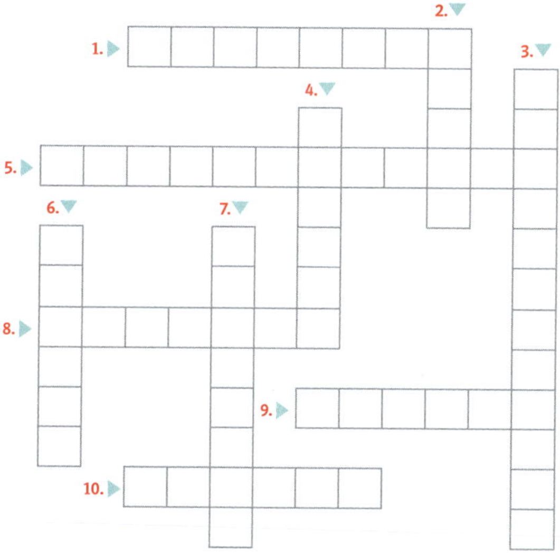

▼ 2. TV and radio are part of the … .
3. build something, especially roads, buildings or bridges
4. not clever
6. Eating too much sugar can damage your … .
7. South Africa has large amounts of gold and … .

▶ 1. an area on the internet where people can communicate
5. Every country has its own … .
8. Rosa felt … on her first day at the new school.
9. We enjoyed the … show. It was very funny.
10. make something less or smaller in size

9 Find the words and complete the text.

custca	ingrats	testroping
slamtecass	ewn eary	maryrip chools
keat runts	herteachead	peed treahb

Rosa's diary   10 January 1995

It's the ________ ________ and today was my first day at the new ________ ________. Mama held my hand while we walked down the road. I was afraid. I was wearing my new uniform and tried to ignore the people who were ________ at us. Mama said: "Don't let anyone take who you are away from you."

When we reached the school, we could see and hear the white parents who were ________. I didn't look at them, but I heard them screaming "No blacks here!" I took a ________ ________.

I wished I could go to my old school. There were so many students there, we had to ________ ________ to use the classrooms. And the playground was just a bit of dry land with ________ plants. But I liked my ________ and the ________ was a fair and kind man. He looked a bit like Nelson Mandela.

10 Complete the table and the sentences.

a) Complete the table.

Infinitive	Simple past	Present perfect (has/have ...)
1. build	__________	__________
2. go on	__________	__________
3. lead	__________	__________
4. show up	__________	__________
5. sweep	__________	__________
6. take turns	__________	__________

b) Complete the sentences with verbs from a).

1. This is the second time that Paul has _ _ _ _ _ _ _ late for school this week.
2. The tour guide _ _ _ the visitors through the nature reserve.
3. The situation was so difficult that we didn't know how to _ _ _ _.
4. The school was very small, so the children _ _ _ _ _ _ _ _ _ to use the classrooms.

11 Find the words and complete the text.

INTERNET

Nelson Mandela (1918 – 2013)

Nelson Mandela fought ______________________ for most of his life. He spent 27 years of his life in prison on Robben Island near Cape Town. In 1990, after many years of protests at home and abroad, the government was finally forced to let him go. The white government had put him in prison for life, but now he was free. Hope ______________ through the ____________________. People were crying and laughing, and ________________ for Mandela to make their lives better. The ____________________ was amazing. Mandela became South Africa's first ______________ president in 1994 and promised to ________________ a rainbow nation at ______________ with itself and the world. To this day, Mandela is greatly respected and many people call him the father of the ______________.

12 Complete the sentences with the words.

1. rau; grob — The school playground was dry and ________________.

2. Pause machen — Hennie ______________________ before he told Rosa that he thought she was brave.

3. unbeholfen — Hennie felt ________________________ because it was a long time since they had played together as children.

4. sich umdrehen — Rosa ______________ ______________ and saw Hennie.

5. sich jemandem zuwenden — Rosa ______________ ______ Hennie, smiled and said, “Thank you!”

6. tief einatmen — Rosa took a ________ _______________ and walked past the protesters.

●13 Complete the text.

Demonstranten | grauhaarig | hüpfen | schüttelte den Kopf | Rasensprenger | Wilder | ein Schritt nach dem anderen

Rosa: On my first day at Oranje Primary School I had to walk past white ______________. I was terrified. I knew only one boy there: Hennie. Mama had worked for his family and Hennie and I used to play together in the garden. One day we were running under the ________________. We were having fun, screaming, but then Hennie's father came home early. He shouted at him for running around like a ________________. I didn't go to his house after that. Anyway, when some children made fun of me in school, Hennie shouted at them to leave me alone.
He ______________ _________ ______________ and smiled, and then he showed me the way to the playground. I could see children playing and ________________ there. It was so different to my old school!
I was the only black girl in the school. It was hard, but I knew it was the right thing. I remember watching Mandela – this ____________________ man with his warm, smiling face – saying that he wanted every child to be in school. More black children soon came to the school. It was like Mama always said: one ___________ _______ _______ ___________.

Unit 4 Living in Hong Kong

Way in

p. 68	**pro** [prəʊ]	Pro; Vorteil
	con [kɒn]	Kontra; Nachteil
	mall [mɔ:l]	Einkaufszentrum
	electronic [ˌelek'trɒnɪk]	elektronisch
	goods *(pl)* [gʊdz]	Waren; Güter; Geräte
	stall [stɔ:l]	Stand; Bude
	noodle ['nu:dl]	Nudel
	to **taste** [teɪst]	schmecken
p. 69	**pollution** [pə'lu:ʃn]	Verschmutzung
	thick [θɪk]	dick
	smog [smɒg]	Smog
	health [helθ]	Gesundheits-; gesundheitlich
	martial art [ˌmɑ:ʃl‿'ɑ:t]	Kampfkunst; Kampfsportart
	media ['mi:diə]	Medien-
	mixture ['mɪkstʃə]	Mischung
	to **relax** [rɪ'læks]	sich entspannen; sich ausruhen
	scale [skeɪl]	Skala; Maßstab; Ausmaß
	hurry ['hʌri]	Eile; Hast
	bank [bæŋk]	Bank
	pressure ['preʃə]	Druck

Station 1

Buying and selling

to **browse** [braʊz]	durchstöbern
latest ['leɪtɪst]	neueste
brand-new [ˌbrænd'nju:]	brandneu
original [ə'rɪdʒnl]	original; ursprünglich
to **resell** [ˌri:'sel]	wiederverkaufen; weiterverkaufen
to **swap** [swɒp]	tauschen

to **afford** [ə'fɔ:d]	sich leisten
to **bargain** ['bɑ:gɪn]	(ver)handeln
to **purchase** ['pɜ:tʃəs]	kaufen; erwerben
to **stock** [stɒk]	führen; vorrätig haben
offer ['ɒfə]	Angebot
to **waste** [weɪst]	verschwenden
second-hand [ˌseknd'hænd]	gebraucht; secondhand; aus zweiter Hand
to **contact** ['kɒntækt]	sich in Verbindung setzen; kontaktieren
discount ['dɪskaʊnt]	Rabatt; Preisnachlass

p. 70	**sneakerhead** ['sni:kəhed]	*Sammler von Sportschuhen*
	rare [reə]	rar; selten
	pair [peə]	Paar
	heart [hɑ:t]	Herz; Zentrum
	busy ['bɪzi]	rege; belebt; *hier:* aktiv
	district ['dɪstrɪkt]	Distrikt; Bezirk
	sneaker *(AE)* ['sni:kə]	Sportschuh; Sneaker
	to **camp** [kæmp]	campen; kampieren; zelten
	overnight [ˌəʊvə'naɪt]	über Nacht
	to **claim** [kleɪm]	behaupten; beanspruchen
	to **go crazy** [ˌgəʊ 'kreɪzi]	ausflippen; durchdrehen; verrückt werden
	to **nag sb** [næg]	jmdm. auf die Nerven gehen
	for ages [fər‿'eɪdʒɪz]	ewig lange
	pocket money ['pɒkɪt ˌmʌni]	Taschengeld
	grown-up [ˌgrəʊn‿'ʌp]	Erwachsener; Erwachsene
	to **keep a record of sth** [ˌki:p‿ə 'rekɔ:d‿əv]	über etw. Buch führen
	twice [twaɪs]	zweimal; doppelt
	to **guess** [ges]	annehmen; vermuten; schätzen
p. 71	**the poor** [ðə 'pɔ:]	die Armen

Station 2

Verbs for effects

to **do sth about sth** [ˌduː əˈbaʊt]	etw. gegen etw. unternehmen
to **produce** [prəˈdjuːs]	erzeugen; herstellen; anbauen
to **increase** [ɪnˈkriːs]	erhöhen; steigern
to **improve** [ɪmˈpruːv]	verbessern
to **decrease** [dɪˈkriːs]	vermindern; abnehmen
to **raise** [reɪz]	anheben; erhöhen
to **generate** [ˈdʒenreɪt]	generieren; erzeugen
to **alter** [ˈɔːltə]	(ver)ändern

p. 74	**host** [həʊst]	Talkmaster; Gastgeber; Gastgeberin
	conversation [ˌkɒnvəˈseɪʃn]	Konversation; Gespräch; Unterhaltung
	renewable energy [rɪˌnjuːəbl‿ˈenədʒi]	erneuerbare Energie
	not at all [ˌnɒt‿ət‿ˈɔːl]	überhaupt nicht; gar nicht
	power plant [ˈpaʊə ˌplɑːnt]	Kraftwerk
	to **get worse** [ˌget ˈwɜːs]	schlimmer werden
	technology [tekˈnɒlədʒi]	Technologie
	instead of [ɪnˈsted‿əv]	statt; anstatt; an Stelle von
	bath [bɑːθ]	Bad; Badewanne
	eco-friendly [ˈiːkəʊˌfrendli]	umweltfreundlich
	solar panel [ˌsəʊlə ˈpænl]	Sonnenkollektor
	roof [ruːf]	Dach
	motion sensor [ˌməʊʃn ˈsensə]	Bewegungsmelder
	light [laɪt]	Licht; Lampe
	to **go on** [ˌgəʊ‿ˈɒn]	angehen
	development [dɪˈveləpmənt]	Entwicklung
	transparent [trænˈspærnt]	durchsichtig; transparent

	cell [sel]	Zelle
	exhaust fumes *(pl)* [ɪg'zɔ:st ˌfju:mz]	Abgase *(von Fahrzeugen)*
	pod [pɒd]	*hier:* Gondel; Kabine
	ski lift ['ski: ˌlɪft]	Skilift
	to **carry** ['kæri]	befördern
	quality ['kwɒləti]	Qualität; Eigenschaft; Merkmal
p. 75	**effect** [ɪ'fekt]	Effekt; Wirkung; Auswirkung
p. 76	**aged** [eɪdʒd]	im Alter von
	chart [tʃɑ:t]	Diagramm; Tabelle

Reading corner

p. 78	**truth** [tru:θ]	Wahrheit
	out [aʊt]	draußen; aus; außerhalb
	puzzle ['pʌzl]	Rätsel; Puzzle
	press [pres]	Presse
	to **threaten** ['θretn]	bedrohen
	to **punish** ['pʌnɪʃ]	bestrafen
	journalist ['dʒɜ:nlɪst]	Journalist; Journalistin
	to **publish** ['pʌblɪʃ]	veröffentlichen; publizieren; verlegen
p. 79	**international** [ˌɪntə'næʃnl]	international
	to **censor** ['sensə]	zensieren
	control [kən'trəʊl]	Kontrolle
	publisher ['pʌblɪʃə]	Verlag; Herausgeber
	critical ['krɪtɪkl]	kritisch
	flow [fləʊ]	Fluss; Fließen; Strömung
	to **control** [kən'trəʊl]	kontrollieren
	phrase [freɪz]	Redewendung; Ausdruck; Satz
	democracy [dɪ'mɒkrəsi]	Demokratie
	oppression [ə'preʃn]	Unterdrückung
	human rights *(pl)* [ˌhju:mən 'raɪts]	Menschenrechte *(Pl.)*
	freedom of speech [ˌfri:dəm‿əv 'spi:tʃ]	Redefreiheit

	to **guarantee** [ˌgærn'ti:]	garantieren; gewährleisten
	limit ['lɪmɪt]	Limit; Grenze; Beschränkung
	to **glorify** ['glɔ:rɪfaɪ]	verherrlichen
	right-wing [ˌraɪt'wɪŋ]	rechtsorientiert; Rechts-; rechts-
	extremism [ɪk'stri:mɪzm]	Extremismus
	to **remove** [rɪ'mu:v]	entfernen
	objective [əb'dʒektɪv]	sachlich; objektiv
	terrorist ['terərɪst]	Terrorist; Terroristin
	to **take sth for granted** [ˌteɪk fə 'grɑ:ntɪd]	etw. als selbstverständlich hinnehmen; etw. als gegeben voraussetzen
	source [sɔ:s]	Quelle
	access *(no pl)* ['ækses]	Zugang; Zutritt
	restriction [rɪ'strɪkʃn]	Beschränkung; Einschränkung
p. 78	**available** [ə'veɪləbl]	erhältlich; verfügbar

Film corner

p. 81	**speed limit** ['spi:d ˌlɪmɪt]	Geschwindigkeits-beschränkung
	mph (miles per hour) [ˌempi:'eɪtʃ (ˌmaɪlz pər‿'aʊə)]	kmh (Kilometer pro Stunde)
	floor [flɔ:]	Stockwerk
	on top of [ɒn 'tɒp‿əv]	oben; obendrauf

1 Write the words and find a building.

1. You can buy delicious noodles from one of the many □_ _ _ _ _ at the night market.
2. Hong Kong has problems with pollution and there is often _ _ _ _□ smog.
3. Hong Kong has a _ _ _□ media scene, with a large film industry.
4. □_ _ _ can cause serious health problems.
5. At the night market you can bargain for souvenirs, clothes or _ _ _□_ _ _ _ _ _ goods.
6. There are _□_ _ and _ _ _ _ to living in a big city like Hong Kong.
7. A lot of _ _ _ _ _ _ _ □_ _ _ films are made in Hong Kong.
8. Like other large cities, Hong Kong has problems with □_ _ _ _ _ _ _ _.
9. The food at the market stalls _ _ _ _□_ great.
10. Hong Kong was a British colony for many years, but is now part of China. It is still an interesting _ _ _ _ _□_ of east and west.

A very tall building in a city: _ _ _ _ _ _ _ _ _ _

2 Find the words and complete the text.

bargaingoodsinternationalmallsnoodlesseafoodstallstastes

INTERNET

Shopping in Hong Kong

If you like shopping, you'll love Hong Kong! Its many shopping ____________ attract lots of ________________ visitors. Don't miss the exciting night markets when you're there. Temple Street night market is at its best from 7 p.m. to 10 p.m., when it's full with ______________ and people.

There you can ________________________ for cool clothes, shoes and electronic _______________. Many of the stalls sell delicious food. You can get anything from simple ____________________ to strange but wonderful ____________________. And it _________________ great!

3 What can you see in the pictures?

1.  ______________________________

2.  ______________________________

3.  ______________________________

4.  ______________________________

4 Write the words in English and German.

1.  ______________ ______________
2.  ______________ ______________
3.  ______________ ______________
4.  ______________ ______________

5 Complete the dialogue.

Kenneth: Where did you get those s_ _ _ _ _ _ _?
I've wanted a p_ _ _ like that f_ _
a_ _ _. They're very r_ _ _!

Cindy: I know. I got them in Sneaker Street, in the
h_ _ _ _ of the shopping d_ _ _ _ _ _ _.
You know it, right?

Kenneth: Yes, of course. It's amazing! Was that pair very
expensive?

Cindy: Yeah. I had to n_ _ my parents and save my
p_ _ _ _ _ m_ _ _ _ for months.

6 Find the words and complete the text.

pingmac | sclami | rear | grovehint
skreanse | wrong-pu | sprai | speek a croder

BLOG

Sneakerheads Blog

Billy Choo has collected ________________ for years and has over 600 ______________. He began collecting the sports shoes when he was twelve. Now that he's a ____________________, Billy's hobby has become his business. He has a shop in Hong Kong's Sneaker Street. "I remember ______________ outside a shop _________________ to buy the latest cool sneakers. I'm glad I did! I wore them all the time." When I asked Billy if he wears all of his 600 pairs of trainers, he said: "Not at the same time!" There are some he wears, but others he keeps in the original box. "I would never sell them," he says. Some kids buy sneakers and resell them at five times the price, but for Billy it's different. "For me, owning the shoes is the fun part," he _______________. He __________ ____ ________________ of all the shoes he owns and he showed me some of them on his smartphone. He owns so many _______________ pairs of sneakers, it's amazing!

7 Write the words in English and German.

1.  ____________ ____________

2.  ____________ ____________

3.  ____________ ____________

4.  ____________ ____________

8 Complete the text.

INTERNET

Hong Kong pollution

Hong Kong air p_ _ _ _ _ _ _ _ has become a major problem in the city, causing serious h_ _ _ _ _ problems. Coal burning p_ _ _ _ p_ _ _ _ _ as well as e_ _ _ _ _ _ f_ _ _ _ from traffic cause most of the terrible air pollution in the city.

When air pollution is at its worst in Hong Kong, it is usually caused by the wind bringing thick s_ _ _ in from China. Often it is so bad, you cannot see the tops of the city's s_ _ _ _ _ _ _ _ _ _. Experts say that using new t_ _ _ _ _ _ _ _ _ and renewable energy will help to improve the q_ _ _ _ _ _ of the air in Hongkong.

9 Find the words.

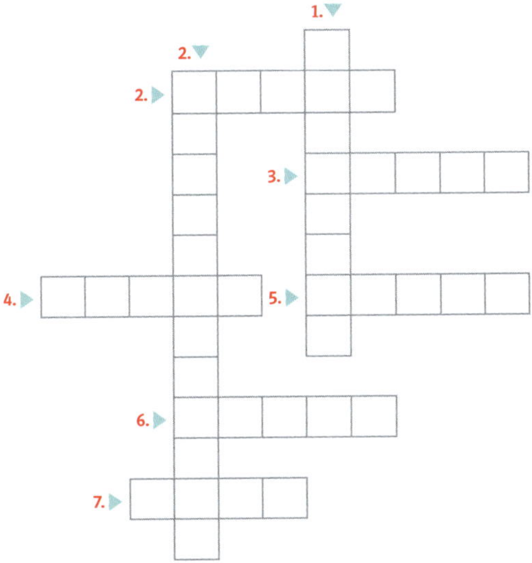

▼

1. I put myself under a lot of … when I have a test.
2. We had an interesting … about pollution.

▶

2. The … shows that 75% of young people recycle bottles.
3. How did you like it, on a … from 1 to 5?
4. I'm sorry, I don't have time at the moment. I'm in a … .
5. At the weekends I like to stay at home and just … .
6. two times
7. Rachel is the … of a TV programme in Hong Kong.

10 Find the words and complete the dialogue.

Zellen | erneuerbare Energie | durchsichtig
Technologie | Sonnenkollektoren | Entwicklungen
Qualität | umweltfreundlich | Verschmutzung

Rachel: Good evening. Tonight, I'm talking to Peter Lai, an engineer and expert on ____________ ____________. I'm going to ask Peter about ____________ and how we can deal with the problem of air ____________ in Hong Kong. Welcome to the show, Peter.

Peter: Thank you, Rachel. It's good to be here.

Rachel: Peter, what can we do to improve the ____________ of our air in Hong Kong?

Peter: Well, we need to use less energy but we also need to increase the amount of clean energy we produce. For example, we can make buildings more ______ – ____________ by putting in ____________ ____________.

Rachel: Are there any new ____________ that could be useful?

Peter: Yes. ____________ solar ____________, that convert light to electricity, can now be used in windows. This is great because, as you know, Hong Kong's skyscrapers have lots of windows.

11 Find the words and complete the text.

Evening News

Free media

In China, information on the internet is ____________ or even ____________. In Hong Kong, however, the situation is different. When Hong Kong was returned to China by the British in 1997, the Chinese government ____________ freedom of the ____________ and other media. This means that journalists can ____________ facts and opinions and they won't be ____________ or threatened. This is something democratic societies take for granted. Without ____________ ____ ____________ and of the press, governments can treat their people badly. In the last few years, China has begun to increase its control over the news and ____________ in Hong Kong. Some journalists who were ____________ of the Chinese government have been attacked on the streets. Now, many are afraid to write what they believe to be true.

12 Complete the dialogue.

kritisch | Beschränkungen | Demokratie
sachlich | Menschenrechte | Quellen
Zugang | Redewendungen | Terroristen
als selbstverständlich hinnehmen

James: I just read an article about China and how the government controls information. It even closes internet sites that it sees as a danger to the system.

Marie: Oh, I know. There are so many ________________.
There are even certain words or ________________ that the government doesn't allow. Words like '________________' and '________________ ________________'.

James: It's crazy, isn't it? And we just ____________ freedom of speech ______ ________________.

Marie: I know, but the media isn't always ________________ and it can influence the way people think. Like the way the media scare people after ________________ attacks.

James: Well, now we have ________________ to all sorts of ________________, so we have to be ________________ of information and opinions.

Marie: Oh, absolutely! I agree.

•13 Complete the sentences with the words.

1. **Verlag; Herausgeber** Some ______________ of books that were critical of the government simply disappeared.
2. **Fluss** The government also controls the ______________ of information on the internet.
3. **Unterdrückung** ______________ is one of the words that the government does not allow.
4. **verherrlichen** It is a good thing that social media companies remove posts that ______________ violence.
5. **Extremismus** There are limits to freedom of speech; right-wing ______________ is forbidden.

14 Complete the dialogue.

Angebot	handeln	Rabatt
führen	kaufen	sich leisten
gebraucht	neueste	verschwenden

Stevie's Mom: What are you doing today, Stevie? Any plans?

Stevie: Yeah, I want to go to the new sneaker store. I'd like to get the ______________ pair of sneakers, but I don't know if they ______________ them.

Stevie's Mom: Can you ________________ a new pair of sneakers?

Stevie: They have a great ____________ this week. You get a free T-shirt with every pair of sneakers you ____________________.

Stevie's Mom: You didn't answer the question.

Stevie: Well, maybe I can ____________________ and get a ____________________.

Stevie's Mom: You know, Stevie, I don't know why you ____________________ your money on the latest trends. When I was your age, I bought ____________________ clothes.

Stevie: But not second-hand shoes, Mom!

Unit 1

1 1. continent, 2. Australian, 3. struggle, 4. Aboriginal, 5. easy-going, 6. Antarctica, 7. koala; the 'outback'

2 1. camel, 2. kangaroo, 3. koala, 4. turtle, 5. whale

3 tour guide, show … around, special, meaning, creatures, people, climb, path

4 1. carpenter – Zimmermann; Zimmerin, 2. nurse – Krankenschwester; Krankenpfleger, 3. electrician – Elektriker; Elektrikerin, 4. tour guide – Reiseleiter; Reiseleiterin

5 destination, skills, experience, send in, application, letter, CV, references

6 certificate, references, efficient, motivated, experience, native speaker, communication, excellent, skills, attached, look forward to

7 skills, candidate, communication, motivated, punctual, permanent, salary, training

8 **a)** 1. a) fähig sein zu, 2. e) sich für etwas interessieren, 3. d) sich freuen auf, 4. c) etwas beachten, 5. b) umgehen mit

b) 1. deal with, 2. pay attention to, 3. be able to, 4. look forward to, 5. care about

9 greatest, wonders, underwater, reefs, Sicily, moon

10 1. dolphin – Delfin, 2. manta ray – Teufelsrochen, 3. crocodile – Krokodil, 4. whale shark – Walhai

11 coral, danger, Climate change, temperatures, creatures, chemicals, pollute, damage, recover

12 1. coral, 2. desert, 3. satellite dish, 4. snorkelling

13 1. emigrate, 2. struggle, 3. explore, 4. offer, 5. behave, 6. send in, 7. take off, 8. stop

14 ▼ 1. boarding school, 3. explore, 4. necessary, 6. disease, 8. few

▶ 2. government, 5. realise, 7. law, 9. waste, 10. close

● **15** ecosystem, bleaching, algae, threat, scientists, extinct

● **16** 1. preschool, 2. call centre, 3. uncertain, 4. such, 5. all the people

Unit 2

1 1. autumn, 2. hurricane, 3. role model, 4. hopping, 5. Trinidad, 6. descendant, 7. sand, 8. colony; tropical

2 1. shipwreck, 2. sand, 3. seafood, 4. island

3 1. the Bahamas, 2. Cuba, 3. Jamaica, 4. Barbados, 5. Trinidad

4 1. pirate – Seeräuber; Seeräuberin, 2. musician – Musiker; Musikerin, 3. diving – tauchen, 4. prisoner – Gefangener; Gefangene

5 the Caribbean, sand, beauty, breath away, colony, all the, descendants, tourist industry

6 hopping, discover, extraordinary, Last night, dive, beginner, party, seafood, shipwreck, terrified

7 a) 1. c) sich beteiligen, 2. e) entkommen, 3. a) sich outen, 4. b) sich einfallen lassen, 5. d) stattfinden

b) 1. get away, 2. takes place, 3. think of, 4. involved in, 5. came out

8 1. cry, cried, cried, 2. feed, fed, fed, 3. fly open, flew open, flown open, 4. grow, grew, grown, 5. let, let, let, 6. lie, lay, lain, 7. think of, thought of, thought of

9 1. volcano – Vulkan, 2. steelpan – Trommel aus Blech, 3. smile – Lächeln, 4. sky – Himmel

10 nursing, Drugs, everywhere, Violence, shootings, keep strong, counsellor, involved in

11 ▼ 1. statement, 2. art, 4. Furthermore, 5. nearby, 7. goal
▶ 3. distant, 6. departure, 8. return, 9. obviously

12 took place, that time, brutal, ugly, smile, terrified of, punishments, prisoners, hunted

13 1. continue, 2. cry, 3. discover, 4. fire, 5. get away from, 6. open, 7. recognise, 8. wonder

● 14 cabin, evil, dagger, walk the plank, governess, fool, shoot

L

Unit 3

1 1. apartheid, 2. territory, 3. Nelson Mandela, 4. townships, 5. South African, 6. nature reserve, 7. diamonds, 8. National Park; Pretoria

2 colony, the Dutch, war, apartheid, separated, democratic elections, build, nation, gated communities, townships

3 1. hunter, 2. crash, 3. guard, 4. ranger

4 crash, face injuries, suffered, treatment, questioning

5 Dear Sir or Madam, crash, guilty, fault, nightmares, treatment, go on, Yours faithfully

6 1. lion – Löwe, 2. rhino – Nashorn, 3. baboon – Pavian, 4. buffalo – Büffel, 5. leopard – Leopard; Leopardin

7 conserve, game, leopard, buffalo, rangers, deserve, ivory, face, challenges, reduce, poaching

8 ▼ 2. media, 3. construction, 4. stupid, 6. health, 7. diamonds
▶ 1. chatroom, 5. constitution, 8. awkward, 9. puppet, 10. reduce

9 new year, primary school, staring, protesting, deep breath, take turns, cactus, classmates, headteacher

10 a) 1. build, built, built, 2. go on, went on, gone on, 3. lead, led, led, 4. show up, showed up, shown up, 5. sweep, swept, swept, 6. take turns, took turns, taken turns
b) 1. shown up, 2. led, 3. go on, 4. took turns

11 apartheid, swept, townships, praying, atmosphere, black, build, peace, nation

12 1. rough, 2. paused, 3. awkward, 4. turned around, 5. turned to, 6. deep breath

● 13 protesters, sprinkler, savage, shook his head, skipping, grey-haired, step at a time

Unit 4

1 1. stalls, 2. thick, 3. busy, 4. Smog, 5. electronic, 6. pros and cons, 7. martial arts, 8. pollution, 9. tastes, 10. mixture; skyscraper

2 malls, international, stalls, bargain, goods, noodles, seafood, tastes

3 1. stall, 2. noodles, 3. heart, 4. camp

4 1. sneaker – Sportschuh, 2. bank – Bank, 3. ski lift – Skilift, 4. bath – Badewanne

5 sneakers, pair, for ages, rare, heart, district, nag, pocket money

6 sneakers, pairs, grown-up, camping, overnight, claims, keeps a record, rare

7 1. power plant – Kraftwerk, 2. solar panel – Sonnenkollektor, 3. exhaust fumes – Abgase, 4. roof – Dach

8 pollution, health, power plants, exhaust fumes, smog, skyscrapers, technology, quality

9 ▼ 1. pressure, 2. conversation
▶ 2. chart, 3. scale, 4. hurry, 5. relax, 6. twice, 7. host

10 renewable energy, technology, pollution, quality, eco-friendly, solar panels, developments, Transparent, cells

11 controlled, censored, guaranteed, press, publish, punished, freedom of speech, media, critical

12 restrictions, phrases, democracy, human rights, take … for granted, objective, terrorist, access, sources, critical

● 13 1. publishers, 2. flow, 3. Oppression, 4. glorify, 5. extremism

● 14 latest, stock, afford, offer, purchase, bargain, discount, waste, second-hand

Notizen

Notizen